BOOKS BY EDMUND BERRIGAN

We'll All Go Together (Fewer & Further Editions, 2015)

Can It! (Letter Machine Editions, 2013)

Glad Stone Children (Farfalla, McMillan and Parrish, 2008)

Your Cheatin' Heart (Furniture Press, 2004)

Disarming Matter (Owl Press, 1999)

MORE GONE

CITY LIGHTS SPOTLIGHT SERIES NO. 18

EDMUND BERRIGAN

MORE

GONE

CITY LIGHTS

SAN FRANCISCO

CITY LIGHTS SPOTLIGHT
The City Lights Spotlight Series was founded in 2009,
and is edited by Garrett Caples.

Library of Congress Cataloging-in-Publication Data
Names: Berrigan, Edmund, 1974- author.
Title: More gone / poems by Edmund Berrigan.
Description: San Francisco : City Lights, [2019] | Series: City Lights
spotlight series ; no. 15
Identifiers: LCCN 2018057265 | ISBN 9780872867666
Subjects: LCSH: Cities and towns—Poetry. | American poetry—21st century.
Classification: LCC PS3602.E76353 A6 2019 | DDC 811/.6—dc23
LC record available at https://lccn.loc.gov/2018057265

Cover art: Blue/Cigarettes [detail] by George Schneeman
Copyright © 2001 by The Estate of George Schneeman.

Some of these poems have appeared in/on/at *20012, Big Bell, Big Bridge, bright
pink mosquito, Fell Swoop, Like Musical Instruments, Ow, Saltgrass, The Day Lady
Gaga Died, The Equalizer 2.0, Mundane Egg, The Recluse, The Volta Book of
Poets*, and *Vlak*. Thanks and praise to the editors for ringing the bells.

All City Lights Books are distributed to the trade by
Consortium Book Sales and Distribution: www.cbsd.com

For small press poetry titles by this author and others,
visit Small Press Distribution: www.spdbooks.com

City Lights Books are published at the City Lights Bookstore,
261 Columbus Avenue, San Francisco, CA 94133
www.citylights.com

CONTENTS

MORE GONE

In my teens

I laid in bed

at night

& wondered

in terror

how my consciousness

could cease

until I slept

STEMS

I.

while walking in lately
    in a perky singe

in search of transportation
    or a postcard of

photo dig the swagger pause
                & drop

with a church organ playing behind
you must accept the hospitality
    of my camp

or

some glimpsed at personality & flash
how did the feeling feel to you

in the morgue you had stood in
that began with a signup
                & ended with a reading

radiator covers with swinging doors
at the
       rebel headquarters

not a bad place to chase a rat into a swell

I was influenced early on by the curl
      on the bottom of the letter 't'
   as my old man drew it

it also amused him to imitate my handwriting
when I was in the single digits
enough to do my homework
once or twice

'tell it what it is'

it can only jump so high
of emotional distress, heroism, or violence

it tends to have daydreams
& is not so into basketball

it likes to sneak down to the bar
to pass the 45 minutes before
the 45 minutes

you fucking pony wind

it was supposed to be meaningless
or a plea for attention

but everyone is somewhat neglected in
these handfuls of perceptions

"the prestige is in the cat"

I cut my teeth on the bitter pill
but a fake detachment offered no help

or breaking down when your sense of comfort
is pierced

one set of problems to put in front of a different one

but confronting your ghosts is rarely as bad
as the tension you build avoiding them
until you run out of things to push against

I might pretend to like the haunt & hang around of it
        or bread myself with them
                that's what it's like when things happen

& besides,
                John just said,
            "it's all just happening"
        then held up a thermometer
        & a battery

"I have a lot to say"

but the order will be my own
        is what this room says to me

II.

to wing on some thread
    soon to be a toothless

whose breath is cannibal
dynamo donning
banged up electricity

scores of discourage or threads
here tonight

just a trick
so as not to be upstaged
a celebration of nerve

one extended motion
followed by blueberries

to troll in the snow

to play football in a coalmine
you may change trains here

snow drifts subdividing matters

during their adventures
                    fail to meet analyst forecasts

I came in in the republic
    come on goatboy, said Annabelle
accept the rights of passage

that's what I was doing
            before every machine in the world
            went into maximum overdrive

you're a good man, sister

Ward Bond skips through our mortal life
I must be going, he says.

Serenity in the NYU library

I wrote my first story
in Hungary in 1764

I was freeing language from language

(runs off to
unwind suppressed threads)

Fake blood pools abound
necks crane

Part of the anti piracy movement

they follow us, we follow us

the cars are slack
in 1648
used as an
absolution fountain

like a typewriter
self calibrating or manual

day or night goes on about the machine

punching the ticket in
                    Cold Spring

packards lamming a joint nowhere

can't exist in a standard house

we gathered for the 2nd annual
duck duels

Stonehouses near a diesel supply
    lawnmowers and fall soccer
in the train station parking lot

what once was the all consuming

 various ideas have dissoluted

kept stalled at room temperature

the security guard is about to get it from a plant

See you in the morning, I hope

I was hoping we could get back to dissecting
                              that Stingray tonight

it's always in the same cupboard

stay tuned on this wavelength

a medicated hit
         opposed by the clothed

         I'm in an uncomfortable space
      carrying out my utility

   who feels the same
         free floating economy

the present moment is just
         a little created for someone like me

I guess a collision of drawbacks

III.

Plastic beams are a guiding light

Mr. Wieners was eager for news
of New York

"It's funny how these cities die
        when we leave them"

  The Mighty tie-in!

"I am living out the logical
conclusion of my books."

My middle name is Joseph
& I swank in the Georgian kerchief
        adsorbing the heart's complaint.

Take it at face value,
　　　some of Robbie's synthetic.

I've got to talk to some horses about some men.

Operating without a net
　　　helps stay the guess

This world will stay empty of you.

But I still like the thrill
　　　of the electric blip.

My preferred religion is the guided tour.
Thus, disarmament.

Pro-gangster with a sense of moral unpredictability.

Let's turn to the movies again:

The promise of a whittled necromonger
          paws at a nostalgia.

"Texas Plant Leak Under Investigation"

I've had the worst luck occasionally
like history repeats itself
          for lack of a diverse repertoire.

Still, the diplomats rollover
          despite the hearty pleas.

Politics is like alchemy
          in that anything can be anything,
even itself in a shiny sameness.

If the wall behind me was spinning,
and I was flying a Fokker Dr 1

Perhaps I would not be wondering so much
          what it means to be doing what I'm doing

Or not doing

HOME

A personal experience of pattern variation
with a little cup on its back
how did you come up with Mercy
lenses of ash and charcoal
A cultural body that resides in the domain of loss
days are a shifting of light
& I'm used through it.
inheritance of opposition
further transitions are also hinted at
we don't equate foreign lives with our own
showed up where everyone seemed to be a port of understanding
an entity of exclamation she recognized within herself
it's a shame I let it hurt me so
celebrity births occur. sleepy works,
an aggressiveness I've never had
sensory records persist
hilarious truths and a gold-
breasted sand piper follow me
an interior landscape full of spectacular diseases
awed that works become true

Home is place of permanent work
an element of contagion pausing the gift
picking up fragments to move

MY INEXPENSIVE LIFE

"When I was a kid, two ice packs, three kids claiming to be
    princesses,
vexations and melancholies, the infamous takedown, chickens and
    dogs astray,
a wolf attacked, holy tortillas, the downfall of humanity, the wonder
of the Grand Canyon, thin wrists, I died 212 times."

MOM AND DAD IN A PHOTO

a tiny blue metal race car grandma
gave to me when I was 32. There's
an obelisk now in Skeleton Canyon.
Maybe you're too close to the speaker.
Tell the Arthur Lee of Love confrontation
story. The tender does not approve of our
vulgarity. Double vocal for airports,
weekends and holidays. Numb grids
that represent human inaction. An incidental
arrival? Why that landing? The speaker of
the poem seems baffled to be in his/her
time continuum. Blind Willie McTell, Blind
Willie Johnson, playing together on the street corner.
Turn down the harp and make it feel more
distant. The next few minutes could hardly
be identified as words. A few fireman later,
the benefit of a lifelong love was clear. A locus
Of abnormal sensation. Harder to keep an
indiscriminate man from slaughter. Off state

extemporaneous crushed weight. Consulting
the at-bats for ideas of speed. I will be home
when my shirt is too dirty to wear.

SOME ANCESTOR OF MINE

AFTER MARINA TSVETAEVA

Some ancestor of mine
       probably spilled ashes all over himself
clumsy sot, while protracting a curve
       against the abysmal specter of infinite life.
This ancestor of mine kept a flock
       of pigeons tucked between his legs.
While the sky wept acid he slept under the bride
       waiting for the day she would stand up inside of him.
If he could only weep he thought, but he wept every day.

       He was a fuse; he wept locusts into a jar.
Cherry trees grew out of his collared boasts.

       That he was doubled was inevitable, but if
ever there was a bucket to the well some oaf
       would draw from its over agitation,
looking to spill blood from the air.

       That ancestor of mine spoke through a prism,
but couldn't tell his speech from the ankles it shattered.

       Failure was the only vindication for this kind of comfort,
starving its puppets with rain water.

POEM

I was pregnant with Eddie.
Where were you? I was in England
You had to really punch through
The machine wasn't friendly
I've always had it on the wall
With a little cup on the back
The house I lived in until I was 4 years old
I was really happy when I was 4
Physiological senses I didn't understand
He was really good at finding used English
I could see where there were holes

                    and I would fill them

I went there to be a fiction writer
I wrote a set of limitations
I could never tell the middle of jokes

"BEFORE ME IS A BOOK-MADE CONTINENT"

Before me is a book-made continent
My uncle took three turns at it
A dentist in Arkansas with a bloodied stance
He said Eddie stay home, while homes bury
Til your faith is a stone's throw in exile
And toss it out into the snow to see it smoke
My brother was tucked in a blanket pocket
While we played berserk for kilomonger pals
A model of ourselves was how we saved it
With dust, which was cobbled until tomorrow
Was todayful with spot compensation
Tumbling out from my jaw into nethers
I preferred to stay home threading the baskets
Everywhere at once translating myself
Into larger internal organizations
Compensation withheld

POEM FOR JESS

I have inherited a kingdom of nothing
& I would and do share this with you
as the great gift. To turn in bed,
turning again, tracing the morning glories
up the cable wire, chasing cats up and down
the apartment, piling clothes
by the front door. It's your birthday
soon (7 months) and mine in a few days.
I will be half 70, looking for my merits
In standing procedure, resting on the
Couch with my favorite accoutrements,
Books and papers piled in all the rooms,
Guitars falling through the corners
And shaky hands picking out the
Melodies. Opening the blinds and waking
up in comfort, waking again and again,
balanced and tottering, in regard,
seamfully and porously contented and coiled

Wake up at 3:45 am in an airport hotel in Tampa
That was two days ago and began the escape
From there in order to make my 10:30 am
Appointment with the New York Dept. of Labor
In Brooklyn and I did — sitting in the waiting
Room at a school child's seat desk filling out
The forms declaring I am ready and able to
Work but now nearly halfway through the poem
It's eight hours later in a different state than
The one I woke up in and finally I
Have birthday breakfast with my babydoll
at 11:45 am — eggs and pancetta on a pizza crust
And now I'm 35 — more Harry Dean Stanton
Than Rimbaud but I'm happy to be an unemployed
Poet again — moving through the streets
At odd hours for odd jobs — rereading the
Works I twittered around 15 years ago while
Waiting to be what I am now: unimpressed
And anxious, patient and sentient but perplexed,
With a goofy smile and hoping never to work again,

Even as I work now to secure a future job,
And lay back on an old man's couch
Dreaming of reaching for that ball of gold
So I can chuck it out the window.

BEULAH IS FLYING

Beulah flying through the universe
is not afraid of it, what could you do
about making room from living land
company is all that matters, how
you treat friendship or strangers
Bessie sings that's why I'm sinful as
can be, Beulah sings the Mojave corn
blessing, 93, in bed at the Riverside Rehab
she retired at 70 all those years paying
taxes her hospice care was cut
but she found a landing zone
Beulah drifting through between-worlds
I don't want her to suffer but I know
that cause is negligible and will come
I will learn from her dignity
there is no other way
I will gather rocks from the gully
find seashells in the desert
outside the rehab, inside
through the screened door I see

for the first time a roadrunner
identified by mom from the crest
atop its head, it hops off the railing
and returns to the desert.

POEM

When I was younger I was just as amorphous
as syrup in the sand I was a zero type roundhouse
about the squalor and lugubrious but gentle
most of the time anyway so I thought
but that didn't work out at all the way we planned
or did it but sitting here in this room looking into this window
again seems an equal experience and everything else
a set of fears mostly run on replacements by now
it's always about survival and the nervous animal thing
I've gotten plainly rather used to it
and I don't mind the failing curls splitting down the sides
the deep hacks into the sense of opponent trembled out
mailed into the contour discussions tried into being life
of the parsimony spin it out shake that shit shake it
right out that rigor mortis right on out of this plane
the large print giveth and the small print taketh away

COME A-KNOCKING

His nuance knelt demiclad.
it was an earache in the crumbs
we thumbed a lot of pages looking
for Antartica Soda, but never did fine
never did fine never need winding
amiable stratospheres for a skyfall
a thinking way to vital dispatch
if it only could move along obnoxious
spirals in ovals and milk operas
whisper O sweet nothing, they ain't got nothing
do you think they'll ever, ever be a time when
we don't have to speak through this door?
I dunno, I'm gonna go ask my mom.

THE AGONISTS

Everyone began dying and the threads
unwound one after another.
everything'd seem fine and I'd find these pockets
of lonely daydream. I'd read my dad's
books looking to find out who he was
or what he felt. I'd look for
my sister in an empty suitcase.

We had left places of confiscated clutter
whose weaving into song shouldered
rust over prosperity.
pearls clipped cupidity, cutting us away.
Recoverers of stains unfolding bold blood
solves and muttering afterthoughts

O tectonic plates, my precedents
echoes like bells
a warped and static mix tape
a glimpse of the many outcomes
getting older and trying to stay young

not being able to tell the difference when it mattered
he called me "a filthy uneducable little drifter
of the plains." Migrants. People came here
with a body of music, firing up their empire agonies.

Our theories were transmographied,
gunned down just outside our father's home
constantly being returned to the present.

I, enigma, fortify breath handsomely
harness all fallible energy here
in my lonesome cubicle of parity.

While I pour my breath a Dr. Pepper
"An engine boils afternoon air above &"
oil pumps, timing belts, cylinder sleeves
mate like crankshafts & reverse their rotation
escaping with a well-timed jump

Replaced with different anomalies of feeling
I rely on sensory input to motion
My advanced standing still. Landscapes withered
While down on the stoop we waited for them to show up,
long overdue, and Dino told us how boring we are.

humungous red rose I choo-choo-choose you
I am as holy as a dinosaur egg, no?
                    we shall not identify
Orders some shoes
                    dream pipes clanging and hissing
a misantiquity you can evolve

don't misjudge the connectives, she said
                    needle point

this sense of identity we have agreed
to inhabit in efforts to be friendly with
an ignorant bend and focus on comet promotion
or sometimes a round weather piques engagement
and bellows comparisons across possibility
elating inordinate details until
swinging fists into the tidal onslaught or
silenced by a patrimony of information

Cynical verbiage and Oswalt falsetto
    await the great, wet change.
  "What's up with that," she says, "I've got to
  go get my cigarettes!" She gets up & leaves

the room, the labrador following,
wobbling enough to be

   studied in revealing detail

Perhaps I am bound to this land by knowledge of it,
   a temperature well below the freezing point
of my fuckups, of which there are numerous.

I violet gumdrop
in thermometer jog,
banging argot
in a fair splash.

Dragon butterfly
babies pop
beaks bellow

mooring in a felt stream
pardoned in ridicule
a volt milieu.

I won't go down in the place I've put me

a green diplomatic bubble recognizant
of its futureless serenity whips
now the march of sand slips
how can we opt enjoined and sculpt
deep in whose widow calcifies the root

I photo keep speak the sweet spleen speak
feather cap mea culpa hurdle
pour deep in the third story

Nothing happens.
hinting countries & lights flickering
drink shadows from daddy longlegs
sunset beaks.

kick it, kick it nostalgically
wrapped up in Great Grandma's blanket,

Fetch some food for the mega fauna
O permissive babbling blow my house
into a spittoon's worth of wended ways.

In felony we soap
knee-deep in exorbitant economy
until a sea of it
not drowned by luck
I would do anything for
but maybe I'm stuck here
I can't just give it all away
I feel your arms inside of me
reaching out from it, placating,

Through the sealed door behind me bus
brakes squeal in the echo chamber stairwell
identity created by actions, a sum storm
        twitching and known
Connecting planes of equal change and atmospheric heaviness
Living on sums, moneyed and nerved, acquiring Maria.

        That should be able to observe
Jack the Ripper disappeared, longer and
foolish. The performer is much like
Jack, bonded with hysteria,
across the airwaves, into people's homes.

We took huge social problems and misidentified them
so that we could do it anyway to anyone.

I awoke as a system of postulants
but preferred a lazy, dissociative method.
I'm glad that I'm lazy, I could've been you
I called them up and invited them to
The movies. My brother and I waited.

 Your glass of poems, turns into ten,
if you drape a pair of pants over hobbled milk money
I'll see you in 1983. You will be decorated for innocence.

My mating gear is magnetic
      Imagination never original
   In the applications we know.
I don't
    Think you can handle it
Disaster tends to strike,
        then I call in the closer.

        I wish I could go back
        angular approaching monitors,

maybe I'd tell myself to do it anyway
that impress in the carnal way.

Kid empty spackling eternity
& inexplicable drives, their reasoning.
pixilated with fears
hedging the political landscape of the country
but a meal will do. After all, I don't want
to spend my whole life grieving.

Once I rode a California Zephyr
the opposite direction
        from absolute sexual mist.
It ended five days ago as a twinge.

It's impossible
placated with tonics
then embarrassment
from over-elevation
I was looming I could not
disguise, added echo & fuzz
gaping at everything at once
inebriated, pine nuts

I wanted to spell it with an X
To maintain pulse against a person with decorative lacing
My friends are confounded or contented and joined
to varying avails. I will paint their ambiguities
on my long shadow of rotating
dispersions & organic selection.

Our own symbiotic spawn

I was raised in a New York City
that killed itself, punk was the death.
Much of my sense of experience
Now will rocket to Memphis

In my early thirties I had the goods.
I was a slim patient too but deceased in capsules.

We had no choice,
reality reserved for red skid marks on skin
while blue veins quiver.

What I like is reduced page size
what I despise is the autocorrect feature.
My mistakes are continuous enough to be handled.

He'd gone out lying after a while.
Not that understanding things will help you
Made from our bones

Why does that seem so odd?
Part of this life has been removed with them,
making us new people.
Traffic victims.
Replace them with loyalties and absence.
Collection of cherry ghosts

I'll go out for a pinto bean tonight with cotton
Coletti sews up the map I've become
what I meant to be which is nothing
I'd swear to in a collection of accidents
feeling less defined and friendly
the circumstances of naming continue.

Placed low on the register take this history.
She lived in some way I never found out about.
I didn't account for my loneliness as a factor
And I never managed quite to see her.

I gather & return to my room. I hit the pipe.
This poem is being and this composition
is the room where we meet
in the grimy metropolitan subspace,
where we match micronauts
and rest permissively in Wyatt.

Compensated by carbon dalliances
As another ill-fated 20 minutes
Has come and pass in said ill-fated cubicle of doom.
I will rock no more a boat, nor crank its didactic tractions
nor cartwheel through financial transactions
Lighten up, Eddie.

San Francisco when I was still doing
Certain things for the know completely
Fictitious and the balance gotten now I suspect
    suspicions lie in tactile heavens
and deep into Darth Sasquatch
        Many manifestations of natures
Liar moments decay

it's ok to be fragile, sort of standing
held idle by law or language. I think of luck
as lying on this ray of light

EN LA TIERRA MEXICANA

If Miss me a loop,
I reply with bullets;
If Miss me a cry,
in the Middle I remove them.
Back in the trenches
Beyond wherever,
I game Denver
for my Pavilion.

MAINFRAME DESPOT BLUES

I'd swear there was a wall
I got caught in a job there was a red
sky river tremolo in my throat nod
I couldn't make out the voice bud
Told my talk til it hydroplaned
Scootering "pretty" and "hopscotch"
Within withering but able to relax
Crescendos at a trance I could observe
Aside from "myself" my my so to deny
Talking mechanisms like mojo filters
A bit of Sally estuary pulls on the throat
Michael Michael Michael resting in bike land,
bike bird, bike red-tailed hawk bullied by sparrows
"remind me not to be myself" while
breaking frequencies I found that your help
helped me please welcome please
welcome now the band

MORE GONE

For the hopeless night sky often
Whose charms and harms are confused
When I copy edit the technical
Doory grains hovering in the queen's navel
The pain spills over tiny levies
On the bed ablaze exiting
The dunce crop we surf Cy Ginger
Black market sports surgery
Enemies from the wild plains
Rice rips road or savage sweeps home plate
In the corner bed the agate
Built boats to shoot dem rebels
My gun's steady gonna hold it level
The vehicles I need to continue
My relation, empty fugues
Rise up the flood to notions
Seeded joys refuse to perform
Hypnotized and running
A nice breeze blowing
Not a could in the sky

WEDNESDAY SPECIAL

shoulder use prohibited
the surprise of coco crisp
running low on self-awareness

junk aviators pitch exits
Burlingame—enough of names
practitioner of vulnerable male love poems
with a serious lack of red ninja tape

this was from a period in which
I struggled with empathy—not a lack of
but it was over wrought and a little
self-congratulatory

pine needles going slack

reduced salt area ahead

37.5

The stadium organ spouts family histories
with a cross in the closet fearing its truths
and the sun brings a single fact blocking
muscle rumors' daunting signal static
chief mobile in three windows drags
empathetic and tourmaline road kill skids
over shouters of airbag, the crew of the Pequod
through the whole facial hair of cancer
mouth was clenched and cleansed
all rise inordinate vertebraic acid
spill pilgrimizing and suspicious or
arbitrary paths go by my me when at Plan B
he lost his eye path to a car commercial
thereafter was circumvented by
the everyday common sense of atrocity
which is only my binary heart in stasis

PHILLIP

Banging the argot in a fair splash

I won't go down in this place I've put me

A felt stream pardoned in ridicule.

The chemical industry is ravishing today

Reality reserved for red skid marks.

Blue veins quiver, paw at the dream

Of the railroad. What happened to

The mirrored mooring? Miles says

I should sustain the bogey. I'll go out

For a pinto bean tonight with cotton

sews up maps like a valuable tourniquet

I'd swear to in an accident of purpose.

I'd drape a pair of pants over my hobbled milk money.

You keep telling me I mean something like a stretch mark

with a job, to be great or grating, 45 seconds might as well

be a season, 128, some lone metric that proves

your guilt, soothing response jests from Sunday beaks.

Rest permissively in Wyatt, my long shadow of rotating

dispersion that hurt my chest, embarrassment again

and again, foraging onward.

MARIA LANDO

my sincerest consistency shrieks time appropriate
casually but isn't felt thankfully
eye contact jellyfish bare in the signal cell
o gaseous dielectric model airplane glue
lamb wool fades to cell, creepy transition
ten-trillion worms frozen in the sound
sparrow descends from something
& drinks from my abdomen, contorted
It's never what I think it is, but also is
shallow in the scattering of denser geometry
timidity and weak choice acceptance
calm rationale particularly sideburns
connections stable passing through swiftly
distributed by our fuck it up, thank you
humans tending to the individual react
popping out for color-attentive spot display
maria no tiene tiempo, maria solo trabaja
I'd like to see the inside of my skull too

TROUBADOUR FRIEZE

In units of speech calm drapery Dowels drove down electric
     chancery
warm couldn't warm usury to hear Bess in the cutlery watch yr step
off of cold-blooded spilt upon the glade pinwheel in the dipthong
vented in repeating patterns of lines folding packed indentures
while passing under the bridge sleeplessly and rocking from the
boat ride wanting to meet some method road interviews
stressed critically on glass that we painted onto water
Go go go your Nathan into fields of acid-coated emeralds stark
and redressed emerging from the forest paper pepper of Max's
     brains
couldn't Bobby Murcer the eulogy and he drove in 5 runs
     Croton-Harmon
I've been here before leeching off of a similar sphere Dave Baxter
     no longer
lives in the belt his love used to buy me Pepsi's can't stand the stuff
artificial pond or frog delivery yield and a hand on the oar
holding up the ballerina there are many strange missing to think
     about
and getting there compiled and vague before we gather we feel the
     grouping

of feeling the Peekskill cabbies are in the parking lot waiting train
    tracks
and the noble shed No deduction in the jewelry; no nosedive in the
    smoke;
no filament in the endive; no epistolary jokes; no fauna in the
    outhouse; no foxhole
in the canoe; no caroming; no turmeric powder up the nose; no
    shocks until the white
house grin; no copper until the concentrated kill; no okapi shrill in
    a vacuum;
no separated glisten; no clip clop on the condition; O elemental
    peptide ventriloquist bop
won't you modify my subordinary postulant my astronomy
    bi-nebulant my solemnness
opulent ultimately and trouble free my lexicon shaved in trouba-
    dour frieze

OPEN BAR

The lights in the kitchen were like bells

"Turn on the overhead light"

I don't want to play

We leaned against the fence or climbed over it

We came up to the gate and I passed through it

More heroic victories, keep them or they stop

I'd like to introduce you to a sense of joy

I've always been thin

I'd like to introduce you to Asteroids

Made of ice and hurtling through space

Much like we wuz, especially when asleep

When I say joy I mean complex emotion

The feeling from my belly to my brain

The signal my brain is sending to my hands,

but my hands have other ideas

They shake to feel static

Assisting the grain,

trans subsisting,

until we float away

YOU ARE THE SUBSTANCES

Nervous system vision disturbance

The most blood black

perforation development

Bleeding in the brackets
in therapy

Perforation nausea

Staying closed to incomplete wounds

If you should monitor
medicines death

If you experience
your doctor

caution disfunction

Change your heartbeat

Stable goal purpose

or become pregnant milk

Who experience wound healing

infusion headaches

of sometimes perforation

This bleeding bleeding

some fatality days

of high disorder skin

days without healing

A global incomplete sentinel

Regarding unique health

only decisions

decisions the patient

International Disease Society

insulin zinc suspension

recombinant colony-stimulating factors

The short arm is designated

both the name individual

chromosome

above and below

Placement semicolon space

proposed coagulation

The simplest

megabase megadose

block randomizes

calculated comparing

Hospitalized indicators bootstrap

to determine

those already enrolled

in vacant verification study

DISARTICULATED REMAINS

There was no true steppe

The available pollen data
                    suggested otherwise

                Lenses of ash and charcoal
            holding down skins

                        Painted mammoth mandibles

It is probable that the causation
            here was complex

Regarded as remnants of structure
                fractured in such a way to show
                        the marrow had been excavated

It is possible our soils
                        were destroyed altogether

Cultural significance of this
far flung distribution, if any,
remains unclear.

Painted by spruce in
    the ensuing glacier

    a round "no"

Frequent depositions
    due to water and gravity

      Assemblages of space and time
    occupied during
        the climatic optimum

Its cultural body residues
    reside in the domain of loss

NORTH

FOR ADAM DEGRAFF

just a conduit for tendencies

developed, undeveloped

Yanks Acquire Pudge, Blue Jays Recall Pond

a mess of unparticular construction
up and running, tires in a sack

to cradle a continuing unmolded impulse

worth the sacrifice that's nothing

but a violet forgetfulness that tramples its path

Don't think it into existence, better to let it go
you and I both wouldn't be here if we didn't want to know

Makes me secure about aging

everything appears briefly
through my briefer attentions

when I show someone a poem
and they tell me they don't know what it means

I say it's like the Earth, it means nothing
except that it is,

& is full of shifting misunderstood energies & fortunes
of which one may pick any niche

& consider themselves an expert
of its destruction

"we have a large number of cosmetic effects
that we intend to screen with microbes"

behold, stupid wheel

The 10 greatest pianos:

stuck in the fly of a murder
buddy can you spare a wonderful hammer
a mobile with the Memphis Jones
on the baby's head

an avalanche of Thor
falls inward towards the core

in my self-animated organism thought space

in need of a star wipe

I have 15-2, 15-4, and a pair for 6

& blither blather walking through the wall

small passages process in the interludes

& books walk you through them too

again & again as the pleasure of forgetting dictates

******

How does one recover from

O one just does, a lapse in absence

a lapse in forgetting — some company is just
so suitable until that part of your life passes

& there's no quibbling that will change that

religion — never been there

what does that make you think my fate will be?

I'm susceptible enough to fear and keep it deep in my habits

but there is plenty of time to be afraid

****

Jim armored wrestler wind tourniquet
helps the sea-wolves to habituate

the key to the fancy lunatic!

the hog wheel dips itself in

"Lucy, the doctor, & Jack"

they watched hysterical relics of cubist nonchalance

rolling around in the CO_2 inducing turd fields
on the way to paradise

a place so great no soul has ever
a handy & easy to read guidebook

with maps and illustrations

I've always felt my consciousness
could never cease now that I inhabit it

but I fall asleep easily enough

I wonder if memory is only a function of the

or that you can't fund the fears
of the intricacies of skin

if you don't have it anymore

Sunday afternoon on the "R" train to Sunset Park
then to Union St. for a fiesta...

****

Foil & Red Cloud go to the dentist today
just like me and Jess

They react by cowering, defecating, hissing,
& the occasional spine bite

short works of their own

"Wild life! Amazing!"
said one gender-neutral human to another

I am no longer myself now, I've become another myself

I hardly remember

uncurling

sometimes a co-author of the dictionary
hunches in the clef

tone rockets seep into the order

moving gram-o-phonically

when we break out the old Victrola

big band hours emblazoned inaccurate

where I'm really trying to stay

O gentle leap of faith

come whence I came whence I

huddled in the balmy bath

whence meadow curled in the cat's throat

inkling in safari's font problems

line my lungs with miniature ostriches

O linocut

O sports coat

******

I was a gentleman moth
cured in the molten
while firming the impossible
guarding my personality but why anchor down

an illusion just to be a boiling pot of wasteful action

compiled in efforted responses

while the spinning orb is suspended & we concentrate

our supporting animated matter collections turn Auguste

will the post-conscious state retain knowledge

of the ambiguity of thought or arbitrary rebellions

of the body?

a pigeon's worth

stores of feathers keeping comfortable

it's the middle of the night

so we chase the toys and walk

leap out of bed looking for the toys we dreamt about

garden vs. traipse
podiatrist vs. tsar
sot vs. sot

sleeping in a jar

LITTLE PIECES CONTINUE AS PIECES

A man says I am this, standing on it
a woman says this is unforgivable
this will be destructed or not
a style of moment we have
sometimes we share this
I talk to the taxi driver offer
some directions "I can believe
50% of what you say" he says
and laughs we are both named buddy
great cabbies mutter in foreign
languages and sing to themselves
I keep thinking I am 2 years older
than I am getting farther from
my youth but I am also just in
one extended moment I hope
when I close my eyes you are
still there and so am I
I find you on a street corner
another one is chasing his kid
in that playground the gray kitty

rests nearby how is your extended
moment I asked but now we are
just words going over a bridge
whose shadows make us more
and less clear this grammar is
not something I will pretend to
control or master I have no
project but contention
and the monument is already
there as we fade into it

NORTHERN EXCESS

I walk fast and mumble
with my head turned
bees break on the awning
trucks bounce on the explosion

      That's not a solution
      it's a plot twist
      That's not absolution
      it's just my fist

Kneading the dough
every new day
begins the same as this
in the order of NYC chaos

      But we all know
      who we are
      & where we go

the veneer of this paradise
is bedbugs and parasites
that trout swimming

upstream on Flatbush
is just my sexiness
rounded by the curves
of my favorite glyphs

I punch my heart out
again and again
breathing out
a Jamaican sigh

kick start to get here
& now I'm leaving you
no slim pickens no lurch
uncrossed, I and I

GLOBAL UNTITLED

They worked with urgency
a billion years oxygen
in supported life, the oxygen revolution
thriving in a temperature range
the universe is made of haul tanks, coil ropes,
and chatted with molecular folk (fossils)
cave slime and megafauna hastened
There will be no explosions today
There isn't any gold here either
This is the where of everybody
becomes sellers, old railroad earth
has only a few teeth, a welder, a master
engineer or 10 cents a pound
selling mandarins in the trunk
of global showdown   humanity glitter
hardscrabble supply through the house
stoves that keep people from freezing
in their beds soft nights

SUPER SOAKER

I'll be glad Chester Pennsylvania
Dear theme time radio too mesquite
I've led an evil or so you say, but I'll
Music that sounds like cars
Freddie Finger Fender Fauxpockets
We in sweep step misentangle Gene Vincent
Give me liberty or give me thump thump thump
light growlers returning to pink Audrey pink
You're watching yourself but you're
Too unfair writing papers in the pool
Hall to hear the chaos of people
When you had nothing else to suggest
Except pockets in which you kept
An alarm clock and books, as many
As would fit, that brick red coat
& long hair, in Westchester whatever
in Paris he thought you were available
escaped the closed down metro by hopping
a fence, passed a guy being cuffed
by cops, passed a guy in a car with

mutton chops trying to pick you up, passed
the arm-grabbing guys and a Freddy
Krueger manikin in a sex shop,
made it home to lie down in
the corner bed, odor wafting up from
the bakery below, 2 am, of bread.

INSECURITY BLANKET

Remember how hard it is to be a good person?
When you take it for granted, you fail.

That's when sportsmanship reconfigures its current.
One thing I've never been is alone, offset by

Loneliness. I blame myself for underestimating
The company, though I often preferred that

Of broken people over those untouched by pain.
Them I would forget in constellations of personal violence

Like a side pocket of absinthe, and drinking it,
Never to be seen until plain existence begs a return.

It's the perception of matter transition that can't
Help but draw attention to itself. Equally

Then recasting that perception onto others fuels
Our invisible republics that desubstantiate

Equality in favor of narrative control,
Path inhabitants be damned. Let's infect our

Clients with fuck activism and bone-crushing
Tackles. That's when we will deepen our bullpen

One roster spot at a time. That's when I will
Punch you with a fist of roaches.

CITY LOVE

One of the things you missed last night
was a potato doughnut, who didn't jail
community service. I think that office
is the backyard of one foot out the door,
come through November, but that's no way to live.
They keep turning the wheel like it's
a mind lit up by espresso. One sip of Manhattan
and great uncle Elijah crashes through the window,
pierces my chest with a saber tooth tiger. You move on.
We're both strong willed and independent—sometimes
our ideas seem like counters and it makes us cross.
I need to keep my head in the herd since I ain't
gonna die. An apple orchard is sprouting
from my wound, under my commute.
Mostly, the city is begging for love, grieving,
or telling us to back the fuck off.

DUSK PUBLIC

Dabbling in apple public

Claustrophobia aligns

Parallel to death.

This is my sandy street

where I abstract my youth

with various forms of 30.

Nothing is taken care of but

aggregate fossilized correspondence

to nature's best practices.

I don't abhor a vacuum

up and inside, I keep a

distance I'm loathe to measure.

POEM FOR THE NEW YEAR, 2013

AFTER JOHN DONNE

The streets of Paris are a map in my mind
Of the streets of Paris my mind weathered in
I replace them with loyalties and absence
But also a presence shared now to differentiate
one mind set and replicate another.
The conditions of the previous entries no
Longer apply—sets of sadness and confusion
Replaced with different anomalies of feeling
While I rely on sensory input to motion
My advanced standing still. Landscape withers
The physical drift while matter continues
Neither created nor destroyed, but emotions
Transubstantiate from one corporeal to another,
And there, I do bring the spider love.

FOIL IN THE WIRES

morning   He brags of
his misery   just used to
living off of it   turns up
to blow out that of others
is surprised to be
accused of it   by
another who can't
differentiate   the
distinctions of his inner
variations
maybe it was just a
moment
continues not yet used to
apologizing for his his
and walks the farthest
distance I could
conceive   spilled over
the sienna in a great
tangle   Foil crawled
under it poised to attack

that wild look and furled
brow. dad turned 36 in
'70. not much to do
with 2010. There was a
period of years where I
could only think mom
was 39 (mid-80s). I turn
36 in a couple weeks
just an isolated moment
they purposed
themselves as poets   I
probably wouldn't have
known them other than
where   their faces now
have years   we drank
and smoked a lot
together   already
losing his hair   he had a
crass sense of humor
out of his element
which gave in to the
economic addictions of
& destroyed the

prosperity of   them's
bunch of poor sons of
bitches   whose lifestyle
is destructible as oysters
not that anything was
ever simple that just got
it   lots of winter chess
with Toby   He took
mushrooms with her
they were a couple for a
while   but she stopped
sleeping with him
we made a joke about
buying Waylon
Jennings tickets   panic
attack and started
hyperventilating   I
shouted her name to her
and she snapped out of it
I bought a cassette tape
on St Mark's Place
probably '89 or '90 from
a man named Julius I

wanted to buy a Dylan
album   I'm holding on
to my sense of opacity as
long as I can because
I'm pretty sure that once
I figure it (why the
world so fucked) I'm
gonna totally, tonally
regret knowing   but
didn't know if I'd like it
so I bought a bootleg
from a tour with Tom
Petty   something in his
voice reminded me   one
of my failings is a lack
of imagination   the
universe is composed of
dinky strings propelled
via corkscrew from
where to where so
everything is pretty
much hair from here to
there   one of dad's

voices plus I
remembered hearing
buckets of rain summer
of 2001 we knew from
the beginning she
wouldn't last long
6 pm to 6 am   rekindled
my love of videogames
& enhanced my read of
constant sorrow
any larger or smaller
moment of time
becomes harder to crack
when you're clock
yowling a puny cry for
companionship or later
searching for a corner to
quietly and safely suffer
death   it was a shame to
lose   that small place of
comfort   It must be time
to make all that loose
hair into a new cat or to

write a poem for
Douglas called
Degreeness   at a party
shared space and
conversation
was brief but they
fit fondly into the
constellation sense
of larger individual
awareness
and the common I
that kind of
understanding   of
being alive and a
social agreement   to
the disabled function of
verse where I
tragicomedy in splint
pay no pie glue
solve the riddles of
genuflection   woke up
at intermission   dazed
I've seen Lenny a few

more times
since Purchase but
we haven't kept up
stick with moving away
when you need a new
cradle   did you think
I'd ever   did you think
I'd win   did you
think I could win
34th street to generate a
sense of space   or
never change   his life
mirrored the transition
from one kind to another
He was our conscience
desiring mostly
companionship and
sustenance Foil was a bit
more coy   the rest of the
time was for wild marvel
and when that wasn't
enough I'd go outside
the apartment

tell automatic sleep
tell wool shaven sheep
tell red nested Ned
tell magnum-holstered Fred
tell subway car napping Sam
we're going to be
Frank in stark inception
we're going to calcify
your reflection   strange
things happen   when
the mouth is drawn
when the war was on
when even if I was
standing still   my
subsequent
hymns a vulnerability
into some sense of the
autonomy of adult life
and here I am now
locked into some other
set of corners   listening
to whatever echoes I can
make and catching

glimpses of light in the
corners of my eyes that
I think for a second are
Foil   in a loft I lived in
in Bushwalk   Twiglight
with Chris, Pelican
Tripod more of a conceptual
band with Dustin on
poetry   threads the same
the tiny little form
leaping up opposite side
the opaque door   called
Degreeness   Mama
disappeared   6/17/10
True blue exit status
sticky   but I'm pretty
good at drinking beer
good at housing
disrepair   my new
philosophy is when
it doubt, do it twice
Red Cloud mostly cries
out   Foil never

answered just appeared
in a white blur   paw-
swiping mayhem ensued
was fascinated by the
keys   hitting the ribbon
which occasionally I'd find
in a tangle over the front
of my old manual typewriter
her works involved
destruction
shifting sounds to the
left or right fear
sentenced to subways
transposing
out of ear   I keep being
awkward shapes of
continuity like studying
the cells in the back of
my hand over the
decades Foil arrived in
2003 she was found on
the sidewalk being swept
to the curb by a guy with

a broom threw up on
Jess's chest and
thereafter preferred to
sleep next to Jess   two
halves make a whole
that's cultural warfare &
the accompanying flow
of moral vindictiveness
Foil quickly developed
maybe because she was
reared on the street a
penchant for shifting
movement or anything
that could punch a
teenager $50 on the
roses   Strange things
happen   to get thirsty
when hewing to the right
to live   where the
needle starts clicking
a bizarre prospecting
takes offense at
misunderstanding

favors each lackluster
moment on a head
ambivalent violent
maybe an ethereal
playground for the good
a wastebasket for the bad
and frowns on certain
sexual acting
housework and musical
gizmos   I left out a
basket full of wires and
it reminded me of Foil
tangled up   all those
years later   she was
found by a woman
who later transformed
into a man   who nursed
her to health who
brought her to us
singing nodes aside
I've played all of them
now Peter   except
maybe an autoharp and a

dobro retread the
billiards
no new   sweep glue
in fickle slip stickering
the walls and lampposts
her technique is
surreptitious I went to
the show   we ate pot
brownies got from a
Rasta shop on St Marks
just a German theater
troop   when the lights
went up
Foil in the wires
measuring time by cat
fragility bares outward
to construction workers
but she mostly sat still
variations in scale not
applicable   as if any
moment was definable
any element was just one
dimension a primary

source of happiness
rain on the Fisher Price
record player   70s oranges and
browns   that we used to
own   implies a finality
that I've never
experienced with an
object   a few years later
I bought another cassette
from Julius he shook
my hand and thanked me
for being a good
customer over the years
sending her nightmares
and she woke up one
morning to Foil standing
on her chest   Daddy I
want to be drunk many
days
so bended reeds
and repetitions the same
we crawled out of
that I could relate thrown

back in memory   to
that asphalt schoolyard
with six urban 10-year
olds   how cool it
seemed   to say "killed
by a cobra" paintings at
the Brooklyn Museum
Pay no attention   Two
more people I've known
of and spoken to   have
passed beyond our
perception
Peter, Leslie our actuals

CHIRP HEART INNUENDOS

Chirp Heart, my back taxes, student loans.
the first time I saw melting faces
at the end of Ragged Robin
Lost Ark on the Hang Train
Regurgitating Mortgages Unguided
I was giving a poetry analysis.
The flue was a little loose.
I remember my dad bringing Patch Glut
Tamale Snipe The Miller's Pale
assessment home. My new favorite food
is the Monroe Doctrine sketched
in a lamb rage how to buy any Shit
Sugar Bickers January Forehand on my left. I don't know crank
crack shack eye black exposed jeans Betty
I owe a lot of stubbornness and shyness.
I once mistook a piece of Thomas Wolf for a fictional insect
I'm almost over my 16-year obsession
barely Red Cloud. I've read My Sawdust Epitaphs
Soda Millie, Scythe King Misnomer, Applause Serifs Attack
I was born in England. I've been coveting

a homemade pasta maker. I used to see Melle Mel
at Yankee Stadium, Allen Ginsberg
started criticizing me from the audience
and there's Tupperware Innuendos in the real fight, yes.
I once had a dream of a kind of home other than Stadiums
bleached eye insurrection in the hanging gardens
behind the wallflowers. I am hounded then clucked out.
My hungry big toe bores holes in my sock ditch.
My fatal flaw has always been talking
in my chimney, known to me as a crank.
I remember hiding my face under my grey Ghost blanket
Boston Crème donuts one morning. I'm sitting in a cubicle.
There's chewing gum for phone drives.
Cats are named Foil and Never.

FRIENDLY APPARITIONS

when all of the foils garlic in sisterhood
and the puncture of their punctuality does not remain
as misguided as drastic conclusions 'd butter up
is when the sweet absence saunters to its corner
and refuses to let you put a pill in its mouth
there is no word for wicked in our language
we don't treat others or ourselves that way
we simply fuck it up and wait for accepting apologies
but there's no treatment for knowledge of pain
so we keep singing of the sweet other
the cohort winded brick subtle oeuvre the red cloud
popping in and out for color attentive spot display
and the compound site of her wheel of fortune view
as we head in, you and I in my mind, to the big
fiction that houses concerns among ours and provides
transport from our beginning and end story

The state of the world calls out for poetry to save it. LAWRENCE FERLINGHETTI

CITY LIGHTS SPOTLIGHT SHINES A LIGHT ON THE WEALTH OF INNOVATIVE AMERICAN POETRY BEING WRITTEN TODAY. WE PUBLISH ACCOMPLISHED FIGURES KNOWN IN THE POETRY COMMUNITY AS WELL AS YOUNG EMERGING POETS, USING THE CULTURAL VISIBILITY OF CITY LIGHTS TO BRING THEIR WORK TO A WIDER AUDIENCE. IN DOING SO, WE ALSO HOPE TO DRAW ATTENTION TO THOSE SMALL PRESSES PUBLISHING SUCH AUTHORS. WITH CITY LIGHTS SPOTLIGHT, WE WILL MAINTAIN OUR STANDARD OF INNOVATION AND INCLUSIVENESS BY PUBLISHING HIGHLY ORIGINAL POETRY FROM ACROSS THE CULTURAL SPECTRUM, REFLECTING OUR LONGSTANDING COMMITMENT TO THIS MOST ANCIENT AND STUBBORNLY ENDURING FORM OF ART.

CITY LIGHTS SPOTLIGHT